THE LIFE BEYOND YOUR FEELINGS

Effective ways of mastering your emotions

Laura J. Kessler

INTRODUCTION

Chapter 1:

Turn toward your feelings with acceptance

What Is Emotional Acceptance?

Accepting feelings Is Not relinquishing Yourself to Pain.

Why Do People With BPD Have Trouble Accepting feelings?

Why Accepting feelings Is Helpful

How to Exercise Accepting feelings

Chapter 2:

Identify and label the emotion

Three ways to get a more accurate and precise sense of your feelings.

Chapter 3:

Realize the Evanescence of your feelings

You Can't Force Happiness

Chapter 4:

Inquire and probe

Where Emotional Alarms Come From

Learn How to Deal With Alarms

Chapter 5:

Let go of the need to control your feelings.

Why we Feel the Need to Control
How Attempts to Control Negatively Affect Our Lives
What Can Be Gained By Letting Go of Control
How to Let Go Of Control

Conclusion

INTRODUCTION

The key to overcoming difficult emotions is mindfulness. Let's get real, then. For the utmost of us – myself included – life is fast-paced and chock full of family, relationship, and work stressors. This reality, along with the ever-adding pressures of technology and society, can take a risk on your marriage. As a result, delicate feelings like Anger, confusion, fear, loneliness, and sadness, to name many, can arise. Feelings like these are frequently the most present and essential forces in your life.

The key to overcoming these delicate feelings is mindfulness! Rehearsing mindfulness enables you to calm down and soothe yourself. In this state, you have space to reflect and courteously respond rather than reply.

Following these steps will help you to understand and deal with your delicate feelings in a mindful way.

Chapter 1:

Turn toward your feelings with acceptance

Once you become apprehensive of your emotion, notice where it's in your body. You may feel it as a bellyache, a tightening of your throat, the pounding of your heart, or pressure nearly. Sit with this Anger, anxiety, depression, grief, guilt, sadness, shame, or whatever emotion you're passing. Come apprehensive of it, and don't ignore it. However, get up and walk around or get a mug of tea, If this is delicate.

The key, then, is not to push the emotion down. Bottling it up outside will only beget it to bubble over and explode latterly, performing in more delicate feelings or a complete emotional arrestment. Hear your soft surfaces. They're trying to help you wake up to what's going on before a significant extremity occurs. It's tough to deal with painful, extreme, and occasionally indeed, scary feelings. Accepting your feelings can help ease your emotion regulation, lead to smaller mood swings, and ease emotional balance.

People with frame personality complaints(BPD) and other psychiatric diseases that involve violent emotional gists have trouble accepting feelings. They may engage in harmful actions to avoid passing those painful passions.

What Is Emotional Acceptance?

Frequently when you have an uncomfortable feeling similar to sadness, fear, or shame, your first response is to reject that feeling. However, you might tell yourself that you do not want to witness it If it feels like a" bad" feeling. As a result, you may also do something to relieve the feeling. This might involve pushing it down or using medicines or alcohol to feel better.

No one wants to walk around feeling emotional pain all the time, but when you reject your feelings, you may worsen the effects. Emotions serve colourful purposes, including furnishing helpful information about the world. This means that relieving or pushing down feelings isn't a stylish idea. An intention to push down or stifle your feelings is learning to accept your emotional guests. This is known as emotional acceptance.

No one wants to walk around feeling emotional pain all the time, but when you reject your feelings, you may worsen the effects. Emotions serve various purposes, including furnishing helpful information about the world. This means that relieving or pushing down feelings isn't a stylish idea.

An intention to push down or stifle your feelings is learning to accept your emotional gests. Getting means you exercise, allowing your emotions to be what they're without judging them or trying to change them.

Accepting feelings Is Not relinquishing Yourself to Pain.

It's essential to make the distinction between acceptance and abdication. Accepting feelings doesn't mean surrendering to constantly feeling terrible or wallowing in pain. It also does not mean that you hold on to painful feelings or try to push yourself to witness emotional torture.

As a conceit for acceptance, imagine that you're a dogface who has fought a long battle with your feelings. Acceptance is putting down your munitions and walking down from the fight. You aren't relinquishing yourself to be beaten up by your passions. Instead, you're simply letting go of the struggle.

In some ways, accepting feelings means also accepting that feelings will change. When you're happy, you must admit that happiness is a short-term condition — you won't always be satisfied. This goes for every emotion, from fear to anxiety to sadness. Passions are transitory and go down within seconds, twinkles, or hours.

Why Do People With BPD Have Trouble Accepting feelings?

There are many reasons why people with BPD (borderline personality disorder), in particular, have trouble accepting feelings, although it's important to note that everyone has difficulty getting feelings occasionally. People with BPD are frequently raised in emotionally vacating surroundings. These are surroundings where passions aren't accepted. Occasionally people with BPD were penalized for expressing desires, or sometimes they were told that they were weak for having crushes. This can lead a person with BPD to have trouble accepting their feelings in adulthood.

People with BPD experience veritably violent feelings, making it harder to accept these passions. People with BPD will frequently describe their hysterical feeling; their feelings will "overwhelm" or "destroy" them. As a result, numerous people with BPD feel veritably agitated by their feelings and are induced they can not to tolerate their passions.

Why Accepting feelings Is Helpful

Why is accepting your feelings helpful? What's the point of acknowledging your emotions, and wouldn't it be easier to get relief from them? Well, no, it isn't easy to get relief from feelings. You have feelings for a reason, so you should not want to relieve them fully. Feelings are part of a complex system that helps you decide what to stay down from and what to approach.

Feelings also help you maintain lasting connections with other people. Ignoring feelings leads to poor decisions- timber. Thus, accepting feelings is helpful because you can learn important information from what you're feeling.

How to Exercise Accepting feelings

Fortunately, you can learn to get better at accepting your feelings. This does not mean that this process is always accessible. Delicate or violent surfaces do not feel veritably good, so your instincts may tell you to avoid them.

However, patient practice can teach you to be more accepting of your feelings. Strategies that can help you come more at understanding and getting your feelings include

Awareness is a practice that focuses on getting more apprehensive of the present moment. A core element of awareness is learning to observe your studies and feelings fully and non-judgmentally.

Contemplation can also help erect mindfulness and acceptance of emotional gests. Awareness, contemplation, or being apprehensive of your internal and external guests, can be extensively helpful as you learn how to accept your feelings. You can try a sitting contemplation and aware breathing exercises.

Psychotherapy can also be beneficial if you have trouble getting feelings. Talk to your croaker or consult an internal health professional for further advice and treatment. Some types of remedies that can be particularly helpful include cognitive behavioural therapy (CBT), dialectical behavior therapy (DBT), acceptance and commitment therapy(ACT), and mindfulness-based stress reduction(MBSR).

While you might feel tempted to avoid feeling negative feelings, doing so tends to make effects worse in the long run. It can also lead to unhealthy managing mechanisms that can hurt your health and well-being. When you learn to accept feelings, you take down their power to hurt you. Erecting this skill can be gruelling, but it can affect better emotional regulation over time.9 If you're floundering with emotional avoidance, talk to your healthcare provider or internal health professional.

When you're feeling a particular emotion, please don't deny it. Acknowledge and accept that the sentiment is present, whether it's anxiety, grief, sadness, or whatever you're passing at that moment. Through aware acceptance, you can embrace delicate passions with compassion, mindfulness, and understanding towards yourself and your mate.

Think of a friend or a loved one who might be having a hard time. What would you say to them? Bring the script of what you would say to them into your mind's eye. Now, say the same thing to yourself "I'm OK. I'm not to condemn. I did the stylish I could." Hold these images and expressions within yourself with loving kindness and compassion. Extend this act of kindness toward yourself and become apprehensive of what's going on within you. This way, you'll gain the power to calm and soothe yourself and your mate.

You'll soon realize that you aren't your Anger, fear, grief, or any other delicate emotion you're feeling. Instead, you'll begin to witness these feelings in a more transitory manner, like shadows that pass by in the sky. Opening yourself up to your emotions allows you to produce a space of mindfulness, curiosity, and expansiveness that you can apply to your relationship and any other aspect of your life.

Chapter 2:

Identify and label the emotion

Rather than saying, "I'm angry", say, "This is truthfulness", or, "This is anxiety." In this way, you're admitting its presence while contemporaneously empowering you to remain detached from it.

When my hubby was in the sanitarium before he passed, I felt a deep sense of query, anxiety, and fear. I demanded to admit and identify the feelings and say to myself, "I know that I'm passing anxiety and fear right now and I don't know what will be, but I'm going to just 'be' with it." Although it remained a harrowing experience, relating and labelling my feelings in this way allowed me to take some of the pain out of what I was feeling. This, in turn, allowed me to stay in the present versus pelting me into the future or enmeshing me in history. Being thrust in either direction would have only caused me to condemn myself. I can imagine how that critical voice would have pealed out, "If only you would have done something different, perhaps there would have been a different outgrowth."

Stress and Anger are the words most constantly used to describe plant negative feelings. It may mask more profound issues that are hard to define!

Labelling our feelings is an essential first step in dealing with them. Still, this is harder than it sounds; numerous of us need help to identify exactly what we feel, and frequently the most egregious marker isn't the most accurate bone.

.

Dealing effectively with feelings is a crucial leadership skill. And naming our emotions — what psychologists call labelling is an essential first step in dealing with them effectively. But it's more complicated than it sounds; numerous of us struggle to identify what exactly we're feeling, and frequently the most egregious marker isn't the most accurate.

There are a variety of reasons why this is so delicate. We've been trained to believe that solid feelings should be suppressed. We've specific (occasionally implied) societal and organizational rules against expressing them. Or we've noway learned a language to directly describe our feelings.

Anger and stress are the feelings we see most in the plant — or at least those are the terms we use for them most constantly. Yet they're frequently masks for deeper passions that we could and should describe in other nuanced and precise ways so that we develop lesser situations of emotional mastery. This critical capability enables us to interact successfully with ourselves and the world.

We need a different nuanced vocabulary for feelings, not just to be more precise, but because inaptly diagnosing our emotions makes us respond incorrectly. However, we'll take a different approach than if we're handling disappointment or anxiety — or we might not address them at each If we suppose we need to attend to Anger.

It's been shown that when people don't admit and address their feelings, they display lower good and further physical symptoms of stress, like headaches. There's a high cost to avoiding our passions. On the wise side, having the correct vocabulary allows us to see the real issue at hand – to take a messy experience, understand it more efficiently, and make a roadmap to address the problem.

Three ways to get a more accurate and precise sense of your feelings.

Broaden your emotional vocabulary

Words Matter. However, take a moment to consider what to call it, If you're passing a solid emotion. But don't stop there once you've linked it; try to come up with two words describing how you're feeling. You might be surprised at the breadth of your feelings or that you've exhumed a more profound emotion buried beneath the more egregious one.

It's inversely essential to do this with "positive" feelings as well as "negative" ones. Being suitable to say that you're agitated about a new job(not just "nervous ") or trusting of a coworker(not just "he's nice"), for illustration, will help you set your intentions for the part of the relationship in a way that's more likely to lead to success down the road.

Consider the intensity of the emotion

We're apt to vault to introductory descriptors like "angry" or "stressed" when our passions are far less extreme. I had a friend, Dennis (not his real name), floundering in his marriage; he constantly described his woman as "angry" and got angry constantly in return. But as the vocabulary map suggests, every emotion comes in various flavours. When we talked about other words for his woman.

Dennis saw that there were times when she was maybe just irked or intolerant. This sapience converted their relationship because he could suddenly see that she wasn't just angry all the time. He could respond to her specific emotion and concern without getting angry. Also, it matters in your tone- assessment of whether you're mad or just grumpy, mournful or just stunned, enraptured or just pleased. As you label your feelings, rate them on a scale of 1- 10. How deeply are you feeling the emotion? How critical is it, or how strong? Does that make you choose a different set of words?

Write it out

James Pennebaker has done 40 times of explorations into the links between jotting and emotional processing. His trials revealed that people who write about emotionally charged occurrences witness a pronounced increase in their physical and internal well-being. Also, in a study of lately laid-off workers, he set up that those who excavated into their passions of demotion, Anger, anxiety, and relationship difficulties were three times more likely to have been reemployed than those in control groups.

These trials also revealed that over time those who wrote about their passions began to develop perceptivity into what those passions meant(or didn't mean!), using expressions similar as "I've learned," "It struck me that," "The reason that," "I now realize," and "I understand." The process of jotting allowed them to gain a new perspective on their feelings and to understand them and their counteraccusations more easily.

Then it's an exercise you can use to reflect through jotting. You could do this every day, but it's beneficial when you're going through a tough time or a big transition, or if you're feeling vigorous fermentation — or if you've had a delicate experience that you suppose you haven't relatively reused.

Set a timekeeper for 20 twinkles

Using a tablet or computer, write about your emotional gests once a week, month, or time. Don't worry about making it perfect or readable; go where your mind takes you. In the end, you don't have to save the document; the point is that those studies are now out of you and on the runner. You can also use these three approaches – broadening your vocabulary, noting the intensity of an emotion, and writing it out – when trying to understand another person's feelings.

By further understanding what they're feeling more precisely, you'll be better equipped to respond productively. Once you understand what you're feeling, you can also address and learn from those more directly described feelings.

Chapter 3:

Realize the Evanescence of your feelings

Every one of your feelings is impermanent. They arise and live within you for a time and also vanish. It's easy to forget this when you're dealing with delicate feelings. Allow yourself to witness and observe your feelings with kind attention and tolerance, giving them the latitude to transubstantiate and, in numerous cases, fully dematerialize.

To embrace this process, ask yourself.

- "What and where is this feeling?"
- "What do I need now?"
- "How can I nurture it?"
- "What can I do for my mate?"
- "What can my mate do for me?"
- "How can we, as a couple, turn toward one another with acts of loving- kindness?"

Asking these focused questions and responding, in turn, will go a long way to promoting empathy, compassion, and connection within your relationship. "The truth is, we all go through cycles of feelings and ultimately return to neutral. We also remain in a neutral state of equilibrium until some encouragement acts on us again, and also we feel an emotion until it too fades down and we return to neutral again."

"The truth is, we all go through cycles of feelings and ultimately return to neutral. We also remain in a neutral state of equilibrium until some encouragement acts on us again, and also we feel an emotion until it too fades down and we return to neutral again."

So the good news is that all unwelcome feelings are impermanent. Passions like Anger, sadness, and unease all ultimately fade down. (They might return, obviously, as in the case of depression. But indeed, in cases of clinical depression or generalized anxiety, there are always moments of pleasure or ease, certainly, if they're veritably subtle or short-lived.) Unfortunately, the other news is that warm feelings like happiness, joy, and pleasure also change and vanish.

No one is genuinely "happy all the time." The truth is we all go through cycles of feelings and ultimately return to neutral. We also remain in a neutral state of equilibrium until some encouragement acts on us again, and also we feel emotion until it too fades down and we return to neutral again. Disappointment and suffering frequently occur when people suppose they should remain happy all the time or repel feeling sad or angry because they think, "I should no way feel worried." Again, the verity is we all go through cycles of feelings in our lives, but if left alone, our feelings fade – indeed, the happy bones and that's OK.

Do your stylish to be aware and apprehensive of your feelings. Fete that they, too, are impermanent. Whatever it's that's giving you joy will ultimately vanish, so be mindful of it, appreciate it, and enjoy the pleasure it brings you, but don't cleave to it and try to make it something that it's not. Refrain from feeling only joy and happiness ever. Whatever it's that's pleasing, you will eventually stop causing you to feel that way, or it will beget you to feel something other than pleasure – either when it disappears or when your nervous system gets affected by the encouragement and gets bored by it.

For illustration, other people in your life will bring you joy, but ultimately your connections with them will also beget disappointment. That's normal. Your favourite effects can also pleasure you, but they are impermanent and will wear out, break, or vanish and beget your disappointment. So, appreciate the persons and effects in your life. Fete that when they disappear or die, there will be pain, loss, and anguish. But also, that acute pain will probably fade over time if you repel adhering to the belief that the physical world should be endless. The flashback that our spiritual connections are eternal indeed if our physical bodies are not. Living an aware life in which you accept Evanescence can consolidate your emotional gests because there's a mindfulness that this moment, this person, or this possession is unique. After all, it's temporary.

Accepting Evanescence in the physical world isn't the same as saying there's no joy in the world, happiness, or positive connections. But it does mean not attaching yourself to the stopgap that any of these effects will last ever. Thus, be in the present moment and enjoy it while it's being! Because it might not be there after.

Moments come and go. Days pass in, turning into weeks, also months, also times. You and the life you lead are constantly changing. Nothing is endless.
Reminding yourself of this is salutary as you defy adversity and as negative feelings come inviting. At some point, nearly all of us experience grief from losing a loved one.

Numerous of us will be in countries of sadness, pain, and anguish over a bifurcation or job termination. And many of us will become unfortunate victims of crimes or wrongdoings. Considering these possibilities doesn't have to be morbid or morose. There's no denying that each of us will witness challenges to our well-being over which we've no control. However, also we're more likely to meet and overcome them If we're suitable to face these situations knowing that nothing is endless.

An external element is enough to raise negative feelings. Evanescence allows people to manage more fluently with trying times. However, neither is anything in it(like one's mate, or children, If someone concludes that life isn't endless.

You Can't Force Happiness

According to Buddhism, attachment is the root of suffering, and it's generally why Evanescence is delicate to sound for numerous people. Rationally accepting that everyone and everything is temporary is a stimulating conception; whether you want to believe it or not, it's true.

It's also important to understand that grasping for positive studies, feelings, and circumstances in life isn't what positive psychology suggests. However, you're missing the point; if you accept the notion of Evanescence but still essay to force happiness and joy into your life.

We can enjoy our lives entirely as long as we understand that negative situations are necessary and none of our guests ever last. Everything in your life, including yourself, has an expiration date.

Chapter 4:

Inquire and probe

Have you ever had a case where you're in a great mood until you encounter something — or someone — that makes you reply emotionally? Maybe it's a memorial of a traumatic event that happened in history or an object that makes you feel irrationally worried. These are called emotional triggers and can be highly gruelling to manage daily. Relating emotional triggers can make a huge difference in keeping you mentally well in stressful situations.

Where Emotional Alarms Come From

Emotional triggers stem from numerous factors that affect people in various ways. What's important to note is that dynamic triggers are unique to each person. These triggers can be told by ones gests, current internal health symptoms, substance use, and indeed global issues like the COVID- 19 epidemic.

Simply put, emotional triggers are events, effects, guests, or potentially people who beget the mind and body to reply. These responses present themselves differently depending on the type of emotional detector. Let's examine the types of emotional triggers below.

Anxiety Triggers

The symptoms of anxiety triggers are stylishly defined by passions of solicitude, discomfort, and apprehension. When notoriety has moments of stress or, in more severe cases, total anxiety diseases, they might have moments of peace that are intruded by different emotional triggers.

Anxiety triggers can be chronic, meaning that they reappear frequently. For illustration, notoriety might have a fear of water. Most of the time, they're suitable to manage this fear because they can remind themselves that they're safe. Still, being near water at a sand or pool party could be an anxiety detector. Or talking to someone on the phone could spark the passion of anxiety. Though these are only exemplifications, they show that any situation that causes extreme stress could be an anxiety detector.

Anger Triggers

With this type of emotional detector, the response due to the sensor generally comes out as Anger or frustration. Numerous times, Anger triggers leave people feeling out of control — they might find that their heart starts pounding and their breathing becomes more shallow. Also, Anger triggers can beget outbursts of obscenity, pitfalls of violence, yelling, and other aggressive actions.

These emotional triggers lead some people to lash out at the ones they love or, indeed, at themselves. Some factors can make Anger triggers more violent and more brutal to control, like using medicines or alcohol. Anger triggers are significant to identify and treat because acting on violent impulses could put you in grave peril.

Trauma Triggers

For people who struggle with post-traumatic stress complaints, trauma triggers are frequently monuments to the dangerous event that they went through. Trauma triggers are prevalent with survivors of abuse and people with hazardous occupations, like stagers in the United States.

There are characteristics of trauma triggers that separate them from other types of emotional stimuli. For starters, people with post-traumatic stress complaints constantly avoid anything that could be a detector. For some people, this means avoiding all crowded spaces or any terrain with loud noises. But trauma triggers also frequently come from dreams, recollections, and flashbacks, which are unanticipated and unpleasant to the people who witness them.

Also, trauma triggers can beget the mind and body to relive the traumatic experience. As a result, trauma triggers might have physical symptoms similar to shaking, puking, or hyperventilating.

Learn How to Deal With Alarms

The first step in dealing with triggers is to be apprehensive of the feelings you witness in response to something. Emotional triggers frequently arise from the five senses, so be worried about the effects that you feel, hear, smell, taste, and touch, as these could lead to an emotional or behavioural response.

Some people use a journal to keep track of their emotional and behavioural responses. Other people exercise awareness to stay predicated in the present moment. With understanding, the thing is fetching when something might be an emotional detector. Also, you can prepare yourself to respond in a way that keeps you and others around you safe.

Maybe most importantly, if you're looking to learn how to deal with triggers, the most effective system is to admit professional internal health treatment. As we learned before, emotional triggers can vary significantly. They only become harder to manage when there are underlying internal health conditions like anxiety, post-traumatic stress complaint, depression, phobias, mood diseases, and more.

After you have calmed and soothed yourself from the impact of your feelings, take a moment to claw profoundly and explore what happened. Ask yourself the following questions.

- "What touched me?"
- "What's causing me to feel this way?"
- "What's the discomfort I'm passing and where is it arising?"
- "Was it as a result of my critical mind, or was it in response to a something my mate said or did?"

Maybe you had a hard day at work or difficulty dealing with your family. Perhaps you feel ungrateful, lonely, or dissociated due to your relations with someone. Whatever the cause or detector, look at it nearly and ask yourself what's passing then. Consider what was said or done and compare it to your values.

- What were your prospects girding the situation?
- What responses or judgments caused you to become angry or anxious?
- Is this a pattern that keeps arising?

Asking yourself these critical questions and probing the root of your delicate feelings will help you gain empathy and sapience into what you're passing.

Taking yourself off autopilot and trusting your deepest, authentic tone to answer these questions about your situation will produce a space to see the effects from a different perspective. This will eventually allow you and your mate to be more present and connected.

Chapter 5:

Let go of the need to control your feelings.

Feeling the need to be in control is natural. It's something we all innately want, and we think best when we know exactly what's going on in all the different areas of our lives. It's important to realize, however, that we can in no way control everything. Trying to do that leads to numerous negative feelings when the effects go differently than how we try to force them.

There are numerous ways to increase your happiness, but one of the most simple and palpable bones is letting go of control. Why should we do that, and how do we indeed begin? We will review everything you need to know about why you should stop trying to control everything in your life and what steps you can take to get there.

Why we Feel the Need to Control

The desire to be suitable to control our surroundings and circumstances is ingrained into our knowledge. This is because the further we know about our world, the safer we feel. On the other hand, the lower we know, the more spooked we think. The need to control is directly embedded in fear — specifically, the fear of what might be outside our control.

How Attempts to Control Negatively Affect Our Lives

It may be natural to want to control everything, but that does not make it healthy. There are numerous ways in which trying to control everything could backfire in the long run. Let's take a look at some of the top ones.

•

Increased Stress And Anxiety

People who try to control everything may witness further stress and anxiety than those who don't. The simple act of feeling out of control when it feels necessary to have it can make a person's blood pressure rise. One study noted that it's further ruinous when effects do not go according to plan for people who feel the need to control than those who feel less need to be in control.

Lower Satisfaction

Feeling the need to be in control and not having it can make us feel displeased. One study stated that" subjects scoring high on a measure of a general desire for control reported advanced situations of discomfort. They perceived the room as further crowded than subjects scoring low on the desire for control at both situations of viscosity."

The very act of feeling a need for control led to a lower affable situation for people for whom that was precedence versus those it wasn't.

Further review

Because there's no way to control everything in life, minding too important about how effects outside your control can lead to increased reviews about everything that happens. After all, when you do not control the issues you want to, it makes sense that you do not like them.

In turn, being more critical can make us more neurotic, creating an endless and twisting cycle in which we get precipitously unhappier with our lives. And a review of others can also be damaging for people who deal with depression and anxiety, leading them to condemn themselves more.

What Can Be Gained By Letting Go of Control

Now that you know how poorly the need for control can impact our lives, it should be no surprise that there's essential to be gained from giving it up. Giving up the need for control is frequently pertained to as surrendering.

One illustration of that's Michael Singer's book" The Surrender Trial," in which the author describes how his life improved when he stopped trying to control everything. These are some benefits of giving up the need to feel control over everything.

Increased Peace And Relaxation

Proponents of surrendering and exercising a practice like Singer speak about the results of increased peace and relaxation. This makes sense when you consider that trying to control everything causes stress and anxiety, as peace and relaxation are contrary.

More Preparedness for the unanticipated

When you're less set on a specific outgrowth to a situation, you will be in a better place to handle whatever the outgrowth is. People who have given up control and surrendered can fluently take whatever surprises life throws at them.

By having a lower attachment, they are more suitable to go with the inflow. This means that still, as life unravels, you will be OK, rather than hanging your sense of OK-ness on specific issues that may be beyond your control.

Enhanced Connections With tone and Others

Since trying to control everything makes you more critical of yourself and others, giving up that control enables you to connect with others in more profound situations. That is because you are not tying your love and acceptance for yourself and others on specific issues.

By letting people be how they are and allowing yourself not to be attached to how every situation turns out, you are suitable to love further freely. This applies both to loving others and yourself.

How to Let Go Of Control

Suppose you've decided you'd rather be at peace and well-connected to others rather than stressed and critical. In that case, you are presumably interested in learning how you can give up the need for control. The tips below will help you get started on this comforting path, but there are numerous other ways you can negotiate it.

Anything you can do that helps you feel more OK with not being in control is excellent. It can be large or small, rehearsed frequently or only in moments of need. We encourage you to try one of the following to guide you on this new trip.

Discern What You Can and Can not Control
There is no way to give up control until you know where in life it's demanded. Take stock of what you have going on. Suppose through the areas of life that are in your control and those that aren't.

Once you've established which falls into each order, commit to treating the situations where you do not or will not have control other than you have been.

This includes decoupling yourself from issues and treating other people when they do not bear you precisely as you want.

It may be helpful to think through the situations you can not control to feel less anxiety about the possible issues. Does your stylist feel settled with each one. As you presume, knowing it's outside your control, you are safe, and you will be OK if the effects still work out.

Exercise awareness

Awareness is about being present. Being in the moment and appreciating everything good as it happens can help you negotiate the feeling of rendition. It enables you to regulate your emotions, especially if you struggle with feeling the need for control. It also reduces stress, which increases the need for control.

Journal

Writing down your passions can be a significant relief for your stressful situations. When you journal, you may be suitable to think through effects more profoundly than if you think about them. For people who need to be in control, journaling can help you work through implicit issues and give you an outlet for those passions without enabling them to amplify and grow.

Get Support From Loved ones

Incipiently, there's no need to go through this process alone! Chances are you have at least one loved one who tries to control everything about life. You can reach out to them and let them know you are on a charge to surrender and give up control. Ask them to join you, and meet or talk with them regularly about how the process is going. The need for control is natural, but it can also make our lives more complicated.

The key to mindfully dealing with your delicate feelings is to let go of your need to control them. Instead, be open to the outgrowth and what unfolds. Step outside yourself and hear what your mate is feeling and what they have to say. You will also gain an in-depth understanding of your feelings and the relations girding them within your relationship.

Conclusion

Mindfully dealing with feelings is hard, and it takes time. Be kind, compassionate, and case with yourself and your mate. You're in this together! As Dr John Gottman has said, "In a good relationship, people get angry, but in a veritably different way. The Marriage Masters see a problem a bit like a soccer ball. They protest around it. It's 'our' problem." We're fortunate that we live in a world where you and your mate can take the time to explore, bandy, and learn about awareness and your feelings. Take nothing for granted, for life is fragile and transitory!

www.ingramcontent.com/pod-product-compliance
Lightning Source LLC
LaVergne TN
LVHW020532160826
845677LV00015B/4016
* 9 7 9 8 3 7 0 0 1 2 1 1 2 *